happy thoughts

happy
thoughts

inspiring lessons for a contented life

www.youaretheauthor.com

Published in the UK in 2003 exclusively for
WHSmith Limited
Greenbridge Road
Swindon SN3 3LD
www.WHSmith.co.uk
by Tangent Publications, an imprint of
Axis Publishing Limited.

Conceived and created by
Axis Publishing Limited
8c Accommodation Road
London NW11 8ED
www.axispublishing.co.uk

Creative Director: Siân Keogh
Editorial Director: Brian Burns
Production Manager: Tim Clarke

ISBN 0–9543620–4–7

2 4 6 8 10 9 7 5 3 1

Printed and bound in China

about this book

Happy Thoughts brings together an inspirational selection of powerful and life-affirming phrases that have in one way or another helped people to live happier lives, and combines them with evocative and gently amusing animal photographs that bring out the full humour and pathos of the human condition.

We all get down in the dumps sometimes, feel demotivated and lose confidence in ourselves. These inspiring examples of wit and wisdom, written by real people based on their own true-life experiences, enable us to focus on the important things in life and rediscover our love of life. As one of the entries so aptly puts it – happiness is not a destination; it is a method of life.

So don't worry, be happy!

about the author

Why have one author when you can have the world? This book has been

compiled using the incredible resource that is the world wide web. From the

many hundreds of contributions that were sent to the website,

www.youaretheauthor.com, we have selected the ones that best sum up what a

happy life is all about – our relationships, success and personal well-being.

   Please continue to send in your special views, feelings and advice about life –

you never know, you too might see your

words of wisdom in print one day!

www.youaretheauthor.com

My natural state is happy.

anon@youaretheauthor.com

The grand essentials
of happiness are:
something to do,
something to love,
and something to
hope for.

After years of thinking the
secret of happiness was somehow
eluding me, I realized it was in
what I did and who I cared
for every day.

anon@youaretheauthor.com

The secret of happiness
is not to expect.

anon@youaretheauthor.com

In order to live
freely and happily
you must sacrifice
boredom.

anon@youaretheauthor.com

To find out what
one is fitted to do,
and to secure an
opportunity to do it,
are the keys to
happiness.

I realized that the easiest way
to enjoy life is to enjoy what you
do every day – not dream
of escaping it.

suphetty76@hotmail.com

Live joyfully and peacefully, knowing that right thoughts and right efforts inevitably bring about right results.

anon@youaretheauthor.com

The doors we open
and close each day
decide the lives we live.

anon@youaretheauthor.com

Do what you can,
with what you have,
where you are.

Welcome anything
that comes to you,
but do not long for
anything else.

After longing for things
I couldn't have, I thought long and
hard and finally saw that I was
happy with what I'd got.

anon@youaretheauthor.com

My riches consist
not in the extent
of my possessions,
but in the fewness
of my wants.

Real riches are
the riches
possessed inside.

Believe that life is worth
living and your belief
will help create the fact.

anon@youaretheauthor.com

Forget regret,
or life is yours to miss.

Be true to your work, your word and your friend.

Being honest all the time
means being happier with yourself
and everything in life.

anon@youaretheauthor.com

If you are patient
in one moment
of anger, you will
escape a hundred
days of sorrow.

anon@youaretheauthor.com

Never look down on anybody unless you are helping him up.

Being kind to others is almost
the greatest kindness you can
do for yourself as well.

anon@youaretheauthor.com

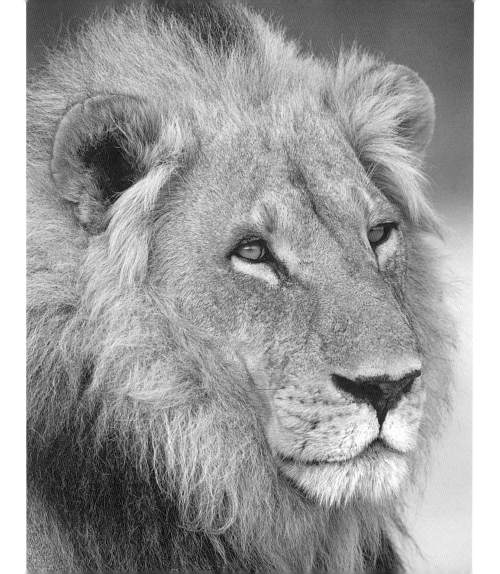

When you are content to be simply yourself and don't compare or compete, everybody will respect you.

anon@youaretheauthor.com

Where there is love, there is life.

When I fell in love,
I started to live like
I'd never lived before.

anon@youaretheauthor.com

When I find myself fading,
I close my eyes and realize
my friends are my energy.

Nobody really needs to be lonely
or face things alone — it's a habit,
and a very bad one too.

anon@youaretheauthor.com

They may forget
what you said, but
they will never
forget how you
made them feel.

anon@youaretheauthor.com

The best way to cheer yourself up is to try to cheer somebody else up.

Laughter is
the shortest
distance between
two people.

anon@youaretheauthor.com

If you don't learn to laugh at troubles, you won't have anything to laugh at when you grow old.

anon@youaretheauthor.com

Nobody ever died
of laughter.

anon@youaretheauthor.com

Nurture your mind with great thoughts.

Once you learn the joy
of reading, a whole world of
discovery opens up and you'll
never look back.

anon@youaretheauthor.com

There is much pleasure
to be gained from
useless knowledge.

anon@youaretheauthor.com

Somewhere, something incredible is waiting to be known.

anon@youaretheauthor.com

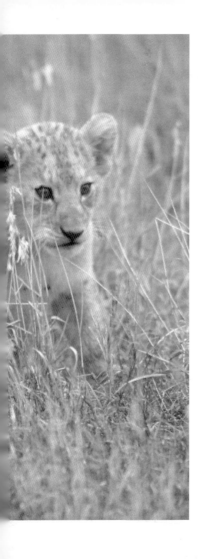

The most beautiful
thing we can
experience is the
mysterious.

anon@youaretheauthor.com

Use what talent you possess; the woods would be very silent if no birds sang except those that sang best.

Everybody should look
inside themselves for the thing
they can do well and they'll
be amazed at the happiness
they discover.

anon@youaretheauthor.com

Teachers open the door, but you must enter by yourself.

Creative minds have always been known to survive any kind of bad training.

anon@youaretheauthor.com

Practice is the best of all instructors.

Never be put off because you
can't do something the
first time — that
happens to everybody.
Never give up; just keep trying.

anon@youaretheauthor.com

Don't let life discourage you; everyone who got where he is had to begin where he was.

Without a struggle, there can be no progress.

Learn to embrace
challenges because they
are a gift in life and not a
difficulty to be avoided.

anon@youaretheauthor.com

One that would have the fruit
must climb the tree.

anon@youaretheauthor.com

Success in almost any
field depends more on
energy and drive than it
does on intelligence.

anon@youaretheauthor.com

To accomplish great things, we must not only act, but also dream; not only plan, but also believe.

All men who have achieved great things have been great dreamers.

When I really believe in my
dreams, I find they come true.

anon@youaretheauthor.com

Don't be afraid to
take a big step.

You can't cross a chasm
in two small jumps.

anon@youaretheauthor.com

Confidence is the hinge on the door to success.

When you learn to
believe in yourself, your
world will open up to you
and you will find your path.

anon@youaretheauthor.com

Only those who dare to
fail greatly can ever
achieve greatly.

anon@youaretheauthor.com

Freedom is not worth having if it does not include the freedom to make mistakes.

anon@youaretheauthor.com

Our greatest glory is
not in never falling,
but in rising every time we fall.

Success seems to be largely a matter of hanging on after others have let go.

It's always too early to quit.

Things that matter in life
always require effort; anything
that matters will never be
that easy, so enjoy it and you
will achieve.

anon@youaretheauthor.com

One thing you
can't recycle is
wasted time.

Let him who would enjoy a good future waste none of his present.

He who controls the past
commands the future.

He who commands the future
conquers the past.

The future belongs to those who believe in the beauty of their dreams.

I say this to myself whenever
I face frustrations; it pulls me
through, puts a smile on my face
and helps me achieve my goals.

anon@youaretheauthor.com

Go confidently in the direction
of your dreams.

Live the life you have imagined.

anon@youaretheauthor.com

Someone who
aims at nothing is
sure to hit it.

anon@youaretheauthor.com

There are no shortcuts to any place worth going.

A journey of a thousand miles begins with a single step.

anon@youaretheauthor.com

Even if you are on the right track, you'll get run over if you just sit there.

anon@youaretheauthor.com

There are many ways of going forward, but only one way of standing still.

Be happy and it will give you the
energy to get what you want in life.

anon@youaretheauthor.com

People take different roads
seeking fulfilment
and happiness.

Just because they're not on
your road doesn't mean
they've gotten lost.

I may not have gone where
I intended to go, but I think
I have ended up where
I intended to be.

anon@youaretheauthor.com

It is good to have
an end to journey
towards, but it is
the journey that
matters in the end.

anon@youaretheauthor.com

The journey is the reward.

The way to be happy is to take pleasure in what you do and how you do it, not in imagining that happiness is some place at the end of the road.

anon@youaretheauthor.com

Happiness is not a destination;
it is a method of life.

anon@youaretheauthor.com